Fishkeeping

Level 7 – Turquoise

Helpful Hints for Reading at Home

The graphemes (written letters) and phonemes (units of sound) used throughout this series are aligned with Letters and Sounds. This offers a consistent approach to learning, whether reading at home or in the classroom.

HERE IS A LIST OF PHONEMES FOR THIS PHASE OF LEARNING. AN EXAMPLE OF THE PRONUNCIATION CAN BE FOUND IN BRACKETS.

Phase 5			
ay (day)	ou (out)	ie (tie)	ea (eat)
oy (boy)	ir (girl)	ue (blue)	aw (saw)
wh (when)	ph (photo)	ew (new)	oe (toe)
au (Paul)	a_e (make)	e_e (these)	i_e (like)
o_e (home)	u_e (rule, cube)		

Phase 5 Alternative Pronunciations of Graphemes			
a (hat, what)	e (bed, she)	i (fin, find)	o (hot, so, other)
u (but, unit)	c (cat, cent)	g (got, giant)	ow (cow, blow)
ie (tied, field)	ea (eat, bread)	er (farmer, herb)	ch (chin, school, chef)
y (yes, by, very)	ou (out, shoulder, could, you)		

HERE ARE SOME WORDS WHICH YOUR CHILD MAY FIND TRICKY.

Phase 5 Tricky Words			
oh	their	people	Mr
Mrs	looked	called	asked
could			

TOP TIPS FOR HELPING YOUR CHILD TO READ:

- Allow children time to break down unfamiliar words into units of sound and then encourage children to string these sounds together to create the word.

- Encourage your child to point out any focus phonics when they are used.

- Read through the book more than once to grow confidence.

- Ask simple questions about the text to assess understanding.

- Encourage children to use illustrations as prompts.

This book focuses on /ow/ and the alternative pronunciations of its grapheme. It is a Turquoise level 7 book band.

Can you sort these words into two groups?
One group has ow as in **crown**.
One group has ow as in **slow**.

tower

cow

owl

tow

grow

arrow

snow

Keeping pet fish might not seem difficult, but there is quite a lot to think about when you own fish.

Not all fish have the same needs, so you need to make sure that each one is cared for in the correct way.

You might think that fish like being in fishbowls, but this is not true. Fishbowls are often too little and can be bad for fish.

Fish need room to swim around. If you plan to have lots of fish, make sure to keep them in a tank that is not crowded.

One more reason that fishbowls are bad is that they do not allow the right amount of air in.

A tank that has no air pumped into it will get stagnant, which will kill the fish. You need a tube that blows a constant flow of air into the tank for the fish.

Air tube

Fish tanks need to be cleaned often. It will not take long for fish to mess up a tank.

Having a powered filter is a good start, but you will still need to wipe it clean now and then.

Filter

You can decorate a tank to make it an interesting home for fish. Add gravel down at the bottom of the tank. Get some plants in there, too.

Gravel

Some fish like to hide, so structures such as towers and rocks with holes in are good to have as well.

It is important that you remember to feed the fish, but just when they need it. Giving fish too much food in one go can be bad for them.

When the tank is clean and the fish are fed, all that is left to do is sit back and enjoy the show!

©2023 **BookLife Publishing Ltd.**
King's Lynn, Norfolk, PE30 4LS, UK

ISBN 978-1-80505-110-7

All rights reserved. Printed in China.
A catalogue record for this book is available from the British Library.

Fishkeeping
Written by Charis Mather
Designed by Lucy Otter

An Introduction to BookLife Readers...

Our Readers have been specifically created in line with the London Institute of Education's approach to book banding and are phonetically decodable and ordered to support each phase of the Letters and Sounds document.

Each book has been created to provide the best possible reading and learning experience. Our aim is to share our love of books with children, providing both emerging readers and prolific page-turners with beautiful books that are guaranteed to provoke interest and learning, regardless of ability.

BOOK BAND GRADED using the Institute of Education's approach to levelling.

PHONETICALLY DECODABLE supporting each phase of Letters and Sounds.

EXERCISES AND QUESTIONS to offer reinforcement and to ascertain comprehension.

CLEAR DESIGN to inspire and provoke engagement, providing the reader with clear visual representations of each non-fiction topic.

AUTHOR INSIGHT:
CHARIS MATHER

Charis Mather is a children's author at BookLife Publishing who has a love for reading and writing. Her studies in linguistics and experiences working with young readers have given her a knack for writing material that suits a range of ages and skill levels. Charis is passionate about producing books that emphasise the fun in reading and is convinced that no matter how much you already know, there is always something new to learn.

PHASE 5
/ow/

This book focuses on /ow/ and the alternative pronunciations of its grapheme. It is a Turquoise level 7 book band.

Image Credits Images are courtesy of Shutterstock.com. With thanks to Getty Images, Thinkstock Photo and iStockphoto. Cover – Macrovector, Vojce, worker. 4–5 – BearFotos, Sergii Figurnyi. 6–7 – New Africa, uventa6. 8–9 – Chaikom, Nohephotos. 10–11 – Chaikom, mariait. 12–13 – Ju Jae-young, Tretyakov Viktor. 14–15 – Frantisek Czanner, Pixel-Shot.